POUND PALS

BY JEFFREY B. FUERST

ILLUSTRATED BY MANUEL KING

MODERN CURRICULUM PRESS

Pearson Learning Group

Dear Muggsy,

The city dog pound, I admit, was no Bow-Wow Hilton. But I miss the old gang, especially your jowly face! What laughs we had! Remember the night of that gale wind when we got the terriers and the hounds to bark out "Camptown Ladies" in two-part harmony? I'll never forget the look on the vet's face when he walked in during "Doo-dah, Doo-dah."

Sigh. It's lonely here on the farm. There's an old horse, Gus, I'd like to get to know. But he'd rather swish his tail at flies than waste his breath on me. He says city dogs are only good for chasing pigeons.

My only "friend" is this flea named Flo. I know she's only clinging to my left ear for free rides and the view. I don't really mind, except that her feelers tickle!

At least my job chasing rabbits and guarding the henhouse keeps me busy. Can you imagine me, who never used to get up until the crack of noon, on the job by sunrise?

It seems like forever since our excursions to the outdoor cafes on the waterfront. Do you recall how we used to roll over and sit up for the tourists? Those were great times, and even better table scraps!

I'd better sign off before my tears smear the ink. Give my regards to Duke and Blackie.

Woofingly yours,
Mitzi

Dear Mitzi,

Stop your crying! Country life sounds like a picnic compared to what happened to me.

Two days after you were adopted, a fancy-schmancy lady waltzed into the dog pound. She smelled like too much pink soap and not enough bacon.

"I'm looking for a special poochie-poo," she said. Then she peered into each cage through this pair of glasses on a stick.

The yipping, yapping, and yowling that followed made me want to howl. But I kept quiet. I was getting used to the place. Sure I missed the thrills we had chasing after fire trucks. But at the pound, I had time to think about important things. You know . . . things like when I was going to eat next . . . what I was going to eat next . . . and what I wished I was going to eat next.

My mistake was daydreaming about the alley behind Wong Foo's Diner. Remember the smell of "Chow Mein Monday"?

I was so busy lapping up imaginary fried rice that I didn't even woof once when the woman came by my cage.

"This one is VERY well-behaved," she said. "And he's cute. I'll take him!"

Cute? CUTE?! Call me slobbering. Call me beastly. Call me tough-as-nails, but don't use the "C" word!

The dogs' barking turned into an outburst of laughter—directed at me! You'd have thought I was in the city hyena pound.

My only escape from the teasing was to go home with the woman. How bad could it be?

Oops! I'm being called. My bath is ready. It's the second one this week!

Your squeaky-clean pal,

Muggsy

Dear Muggsy (or should I say "Cutie-pie"?),

Now you know the truth. You're adorable! I'm glad that a good home has finally found you. Thanks for writing back so soon. I needed cheering up. You won't believe what happened to me the other day.

The local fox came snooping around the henhouse. (His name is Herschel, but everyone calls him Hershie.) I was suspicious because it was Tuesday. Thursday is his usual day to stop by. He's always giving me a song-and-dance about how his family is starving. Could I spare him a few eggs?

I try to be tough, now that I'm a farm dog. I usually give him a "Yeah, right" growl and tell him to hit the road.

But that day he said, "Some storm last night, huh?"

I was tired from playing fetch the previous afternoon. I must have slept right through the storm.

"Rain flooded us out of our hole," continued Hershie. "And those gale winds blew the kits clear across the meadow."

"Here comes the pitch for free eggs," I said to myself quietly. But he just kept talking about the storm.

"Trees are down all over the woods. A huge oak bashed Gus's stable. A roof beam fell and busted up his fetlock—or is it a forelock?" Herschel shook his head. "I get them mixed up. But you know what a broken leg means to a horse."

Gus? Hurt? No, I couldn't believe it! I sprinted over to the stable so fast you'd have thought I was a greyhound, not a schnauzer.

When I got there, Gus was fine. So was his stable.

Oh, no! I had left the henhouse unguarded. When I got back to my post, the fox was gone. So were my two favorite chickens, Myrtle and Sadie.

I've been in the doghouse ever since. Gus is right. I don't belong here. I wish I were back in the old neighborhood.

Mitzi

Dear Mitzi,

So you got outfoxed. Don't be so "ruff" on yourself. (I made a joke. Get it?) You're a smart dog. Do you recall how you saved those baby robins from Rufus the Raccoon? The nest was up in a maple tree. But to throw Rufus off the scent, you went barking up the wrong tree.

Let me tell you. I could use your brains to figure a way out of here. It's not that I'm being treated badly. It's just the opposite. I've got it so good, it makes me nervous. Me! Nervous, for bones' sake!

I have my own bed. I have my own bowl. And I can bark for dinner whenever I want.

But it's a humiliating existence!

Mrs. Uptown insists on calling me "Russell."

"Muggsy!" I bark at her. "Muggsy, Muggsy, Muggsy."

"Russell," she says, "how's my little Snookie-ookums?"

I get so mad, I want to chase my tail.

The worst yet was when we went clothes shopping—for me! I must have tried on every single doggie sweater in the joint. Plaids, stripes, polka-dots! You name it, I modeled it. Why? Because "Mumsie" (that's what I'm supposed to call her, for crying out loud!) wants to show me off to her friends at the Uptown Kennel Club.

   Me a show dog? If that doesn't give you a
good laugh, I've enclosed a few pictures of
"Russell."

   My best,
   Muggsy

P.S. Don't say you heard this from me, but the
green turtleneck isn't bad! Of course, I don't
need those padded shoulders. But don't you
think I look tough?

Dear "Russell,"

Look at the bright side: "Mumsie" *could* call you "Clarence" or "Bon-Bon."

I'm in a good mood now, old pal. But last week I was terribly upset. I decided that the henhouse deserved a guard dog that wasn't such a turkey. So I ran away.

Around sunset, I took off for the woods. But barely a hundred feet in, I stopped in my tracks. Was it guilt? Was it fear? No, it was the noise.

In all my years in the city, I had never been in the woods at dusk. Now you'd think that a forest would grow quiet, even silent, with darkness.

Quite the contrary! That's when a forest comes alive. There's chirping, chittering, cooing, whistling, buzzing, and humming. It's a symphony of sounds! All I could do was lie down on the forest floor and listen.

I forgot about the chickens. I forgot about my old life in the city. The song of the night woods was so soothing and beautiful that it put a smile on my face. I realized that it was my first smile since I left the pound.

Right then, I knew I was in the country to stay. I slept all night in a pile of pine needles. The next morning, I headed right back to the henhouse. I'll show that fox. You'll see.

Love,
Mitzi

Dear Mitzi,

Why did you have to mail that last letter? My eyeballs are gushing. I haven't cried so much since that frightened mailman who gave us fancy steaks retired.

I discovered something new about myself too. In the old days, we roamed the streets free and easy, right? No one told us where to go or what to do. So you might think that a leash would be total misery for a certain bulldog who never had a master.

Try again. A leash hasn't robbed me of freedom at all. It's *given* me freedom.

A leash, I have learned, frees me of the old worries. I know where my next meal is coming from. And I know where I'm going to sleep.

Maybe city life isn't so horrible after all, Mitzi old pal.

After all, I do have this "Mumsie" lady wrapped right around my little paw.

Why, I even have my own sunglasses. I don't know how I did without them before. And I haven't had a fight in over a month! If another dog so much as growls at me, Mumsie goes right after him for me.

I'm just kind of counting my blessings here, you know? I'm never hungry anymore. In fact, my stomach is always rather pleasingly full. I'm even thinking—just thinking, mind you—of what it might be like to get a little finicky about my food.

Yipes! I'm due at Fifi's for my manicure. The dog show is—gulp—next week!

Muggsy (Russell)

Hey, Muggsy!

You knew I could do it, and I did! I outfoxed the fox. How, you might ask? Even if you don't, I'm going to tell you!

Flo the Flea was more excited than usual because the circus was in town. It wasn't the regular circus. It was a flea circus—starring members of her family.

That was one show I was definitely *not* itching to see. If *one* clinging flea's feelers tickle, can you imagine what a dozen would do to me?

Then I got the idea. If I could get that greedy fox into the henhouse and let loose those fleas. . . .

I put up a sign that said, "Nobody Here but Us Chickens" and hid behind the henhouse. Hershie, of course, couldn't resist. He sneaked inside to steal chickens. He ended up inventing a new dance instead!

Best of all, Gus saw the whole thing!

"That scratchy, wiggly fox trot is priceless," he said. "Where's my video camera?"

After we couldn't laugh anymore, we made Hershie promise to never come around the henhouse again. Then we called off the fleas.

That's all for now. Gus invited me to his stable for a lump of sugar.

Dog power!

Mitzi

Dear Mitzi,

Your letters are turning me into a regular Niagara Falls. I was only too glad to read about your victory. But even happy tears can mess up fur, you know! Mumsie had to brush me all over again, not minutes before the dog show.

What a scene at the Uptown Kennel Club!

Each of us strutted our stuff in front of the judges. We walked in circles. We sat. We walked fast. We walked slow. This wasn't exactly rocket science. To be quite honest, it was ridiculous. Why should I care what someone else thinks of me? Then I realized I didn't and I really got into it. Guess what? I won a little something.

It was the "Best Personality" ribbon. Ha! Everyone knows I'm brimming with personality. Why, I've got more personality in my stubby tail than all those other dogs have in their whole bodies, combined.

What the judges overlooked is how CUTE I am. Ah, they wouldn't know a truly cute dog if it jumped up and bit them. But next year, they're going to know. Because that's the award *I'm* going to win.

Bye,
Russell

P.S. Here's a clipping from the paper. I sent one to Duke and Blackie to put up at the pound. Not a bad shot, but my left profile is really my best side.

P.P.S. Don't forget to write back!